The
LOVE POEMS
of
KENNETH
PATCHEN

The Pocket Poets Series : Number 13
CITY LIGHTS BOOKS
San Francisco

The Pocket Poets Series is published by
City Lights Books, 261 Columbus Avenue,
San Francisco 11, California, and distributed nationally
to bookstores by the Paper Editions Corporation.

Distributed in Great Britain and Europe by
The Scorpion Press, 11 Rofant Road, Northwood,
Middlesex, England.

FOR MIRIAM

This selection was made from the following volumes, and the provenance of each poem is recorded in the table of contents by number:

1. ORCHARDS, THRONES & CARAVANS
2. FIRST WILL & TESTAMENT
3. CLOTH OF THE TEMPEST
4. THE DARK KINGDOM
5. WHEN WE WERE HERE TOGETHER
6. PICTURES OF LIFE AND OF DEATH
7. THE TEETH OF THE LION
8. RED WINE & YELLOW HAIR
9. THE FAMOUS BOATING PARTY

Books numbered *two, five, seven, eight,* and *nine* were originally published by New Directions — in 1939, 1957, 1942, 1949, and 1954, respectively. Number *three* was published by Harper & Brothers in 1943; number *four* by Harriss & Givens in 1942; number *six* by Padell Publishers in 1946; and finally, number *one* appeared in a privately subscribed edition by The Print Workshop in 1952.

New printings of numbers *two, three,* and *four* were issued by Padell Publishers in 1946. Numbers *one* and *seven* are at present out of print.

OTHER BOOKS BY KENNETH PATCHEN:

AN ASTONISHED EYE LOOKS OUT OF THE AIR
A SURPRISE FOR THE BAGPIPE-PLAYER
BECAUSE IT IS
BEFORE THE BRAVE
FABLES & OTHER LITTLE TALES
GLORY NEVER GUESSES
HURRAH FOR ANYTHING
MEMOIRS OF A SHY PORNOGRAPHER
PANELS FOR THE WALLS OF HEAVEN
POEMSCAPES
POEMS OF HUMOR & PROTEST
SEE YOU IN THE MORNING
SELECTED POEMS
SLEEPERS AWAKE
THE JOURNAL OF ALBION MOONLIGHT
THEY KEEP RIDING DOWN ALL THE TIME

CONTENTS

FOR MIRIAM

As beautiful as the hands
Of a winter tree
And as holy
Base are they beside thee

As dross beside thee

O green birds
That sing the earth to wakefulness
As tides the sea
Drab are they beside thee

As tinsel beside thee

O pure
And fair as the clouds
Wandering
Over a summer field
They are crass beside thee
The hands
Move through the starhair

As tawdry beside thee

' AS FROTHING WOUNDS OF ROSES '

As frothing wounds of roses
Harry summer over a wintry sea,
So does thy very strangeness
Bring me ever nearer thee

As the cry of the bird-torn wind
Hastens the heart beyond its usual need,
So shalt thy dear loveliness,
Upon the forlorn unrest of my cold will,
Be as that snowy stain the roses bleed

O as flaming wounds of roses
Marry summer to the most wintry sea,
So does thy very woman's separateness
Bring me ever nearer thee

' O MY DARLING TROUBLES HEAVEN WITH HER LOVELINESS '

O my darling troubles heaven
With her loveliness

She is made of such cloth
That the angels cry to see her

Little gods dwell where she moves
And their hands open golden boxes
For me to lie in

She is built of lilies and candy doves
And the youngest star wakens in her hair

She calls me with the music of silver bells
And at night we step into other worlds
Like birds flying through the red and yellow air
Of childhood

O she touches me with the tips of wonder
And the angels cuddle like sleepy kittens
At our side

FALL OF THE EVENING STAR

Speak softly; sun going down
Out of sight. Come near me now.

Dear dying fall of wings as birds
Complain against the gathering dark . . .

Exaggerate the green blood in grass;
The music of leaves scraping space;

Multiply the stillness by one sound;
By one syllable of your name . . .

And all that is little is soon giant,
All that is rare grows in common beauty

To rest with my mouth on your mouth
As somewhere a star falls

And the earth takes it softly, in natural love . . .
Exactly as we take each other . . . and go to sleep.

'SHE IS THE PRETTIEST OF CREATURES'

She is the prettiest of creatures
All like a queen is she

I have made a paper wheel
And I pin it to her dress

We lie together
And it is as nice as music
When you are half-asleep

And then we want to cry because
We are so clean and warm
And sometimes it is raining
And the little drops scuttle
Like the feet of angels on the roof

I have made this poem tonight
And I pin it in her hair

For she is the prettiest of creatures
O all like a strange queen is she

'BE MUSIC, NIGHT'

Be music, night,
That her sleep may go
Where angels have their pale tall choirs

Be a hand, sea,
That her dreams may watch
Thy guidesman touching the green flesh of the world

Be a voice, sky,
That her beauties may be counted
And the stars will tilt their quiet faces
Into the mirror of her loveliness

Be a road, earth,
That her walking may take thee
Where the towns of heaven lift their breathing spires

O be a world and a throne, God,
That her living may find its weather
And the souls of ancient bells in a child's book
Shall lead her into Thy wondrous house

'WE GO OUT TOGETHER INTO THE STARING TOWN'

We go out together into the staring town
And buy cheese and bread and little jugs with
     flowered labels

Everywhere is a tent where we put on our whirl-
     ing show

A great deal has been said of the handless serpents
Which war has set loose in the gay milk of our
     heads

But because you braid your hair and taste like
     honey of heaven
We go together into town and buy wine and
     yellow candles.

' THE SNOW IS DEEP ON THE GROUND '

The snow is deep on the ground.
Always the light falls
Softly down on the hair of my beloved.

This is a good world . . .
And war shall fail.
God shall not forget us.
Who made the snow waits where love is.

The sky moves in its whiteness
Like the withered hand of an old king.
God shall not forget us.
Who made the sky knows of our love.

The snow is beautiful on the ground.
And always the lights of heaven glow
Softly down on the hair of my beloved.

23rd STREET RUNS INTO HEAVEN

You stand near the window as lights wink
On along the street. Somewhere a trolley, taking
Shopgirls and clerks home, clatters through
This before-supper Sabbath. An alley cat cries
To find the garbage cans sealed; newsboys
Begin their murder-into-pennies round.

We are shut in, secure for a little, safe until
Tomorrow. You slip your dress off, roll down
Your stockings, careful against runs. Naked now,
With soft light on soft flesh, you pause
For a moment; turn and face me —
Smile in a way that only women know
Who have lain long with their lover
And are made more virginal.

Our supper is plain but we are very wonderful.

SHE HAD CONCEALED HIM IN A DEEP DARK CAVE,
hewn far in the rock, to which she alone knew the entrance on
the world, and so treacherous and uncertain was the descent
that the law-givers and the villagers passed over his head in
the clear fields above, content to allow him such safety as he
had

Going to bed
And when we have done
Lying quietly together in the dark

Warm houses stand within us
Sleepy angels smile in doorways
Little jewelled horses jolt by without sound
Everyone is rich and no one has money
I can love you Thank God I can love you
All that can happen to us is not known to the guns

Are you awake, darling?
Do not fall asleep yet
To sleep now would seem a way to die so easily
And death is something which poems must be about

But the way our bodies were wings
Flying in and out of each other . . . !

'THIS ROOM HAS MYSTERY LIKE A TRANCE'

This room has mystery like a trance
Of wine; forget-me-nots of you
Are chair and couch, the books your
Fingers touched. And now that you

Are absent here the silence scrapes
A secret rust from everything;
While sudden wreaths of sorrow's
Dust uncover emptiness like halls
To stumble through, and terror falls.

'YOUR NAME INCLUDES THE SHADOW FLIGHT OF BIRDS'

Your name includes the shadow flight of birds
That curve a longing cry near home;
In garden loveliness of cottage smoke
The flowering wings arrest the traffic
Of a sadder prophecy . . . for you
Are bird and summer sky and all
I know of home. Your face awakes a fog
Like blossoms to drape my eyes
In streets where noise and duty are.
And if words I knew to speak your body, then
Flesh of me would have no way to you.

'I KNOW THE HAIR, TISSUE, SKIN'

I know the hair, tissue, skin,
eyes : the lilies, locked and singing
in the bone, growing into your face
and through your face — I know
the pressure of the spirit's skeleton
and point the gentle word ' love ' at it
but beneath the play of tags
on everything, I know my words,
like whiskey in a corpse, to be of little use
to one lost in the golden pasturage
of this ' you ' which is the journey's
drive into the land of a human heaven.

' IT IS A LONELY WALK INTO
THE MIND'S RETREAT '

It is a lonely walk into the mind's retreat.
    Finding
That air is green against the couch of grass;
That water is wooden beneath a ship's hull;
That the spinning petals of a flower,
    held between the fingers,
Are a perfect talking of color;
                and yet, this
Is not more strange or less obscure
Than that each time my eyes
Explore the spreading world in yours,
I do not see, sharp face, the floating
Timbers of Eden washed high
    on the hanging question in mine;
             or that
Each time I touch your body,
Like a mirror held to music,
I do not plant a splitting beauty
Upon the lives of all the things I am.

GEOGRAPHY OF MUSIC

Let me be prodigal as sun in praising you.
I take the peeping angel, frolicking
      in the branches of Time;
The dreamless churchyard on the wings
Of this Gypsy-moth; the face
Within the river's mist; the footsteps
Of this throbbing flower; water's rapture, leaf's
Melody in delirium of sunrise —
I take these things as factions
      in the spirit's lens
Through which I look at you. And yet,
      how can
I trust to word's furniture in moving now
Within the swarm of mountain worlds
Your lightest touch has built for me?
It is the ocean's sound of sorrowing,
It is the wonder of a thousand singing,
It is the world with all loveliness
Lost within the moons and suns of it,
Beloved, that you are.

AND WHAT WITH THE BLUNDERS, *what with the real humor of the address, the end is sure to be attained, that of roarous fun in the roused hamlet or mountain village which pour forth their whole population in a swarm round the amorous orator, down to the baby that can but just tottle and the curs that join in the clamor, mad with ecstasy at the novelty of some noise besides that of trees and the horrible calling of the grass*

We talked of things but all the time we wanted each other
And finally we were silent and I knelt above your body

A closing of eyes
And falling unfalteringly
Over a warm pure country and something crying

When I was a child things being hurt made me sorry
For them but it seemed the way men and women did
And I had not made the world

Coming into it crying
I wanted so not to hurt you
And going out of it like a sudden pouring of salt

Later, being tired and overflowing with tenderness
Girl's body to boy's body lying there
And wondering what it had been

We got to our feet very quietly
So that they would not waken
But we felt their shy, sorrowful look
Upon us as we left them alone there

*   *   *

All things are one thing to the earth
Rayless as a blind leper Blake lies with everyman
And the fat lord sleeps beside his bastard at last

And it doesn't matter, it doesn't mean what we think it does
For we two will never lie there
We shall not be there when death reaches out his dark and
sparkling hands

There are so many little dyings that it doesn't matter
                                    which of them is death.

'BEAUTIFUL YOU ARE'

Cathedral evening, tinkle of candles
On the frosted air
Beautiful you are
Beautiful your eyes, lips, hair

Ah, still they come

Evenings like chalices
Where little roofs and trees drink
Until a rude hand
Shatters them, one by one

O beautiful you are

My own
Land of holiness, unblemished grace
Springtime
In this winter place
O in the candles there
More beautiful
Than any legend's face

Your eyes, your hair

'FOR LOSING HER LOVE ALL WOULD I PROFANE'

For losing her love all would I profane
As a man who washes his heart in filth.
She wakes so whitely at my side,
Her two breasts like bowls of snow
Upon which I put my hands like players
In a child's story of heaven.

For gaining her love all would I protest
As a man who threatens God with murder.
Her lips part sleep's jewelled rain
Like little red boats on a Sunday lake.
I know nothing about men who die
Like beasts in a war-fouled ditch —
My sweet . . .

O God what shall become of us?

AS SHE WAS THUS ALONE IN THE CLEAR MOON-
LIGHT, *Standing Between Rock And Sky, And Scarcely
Seeming To Touch The Earth, Her Dark Locks And Loose
Garments Scattered By The Wind, She Looked Like Some
Giant Spirit Of The Older Time, Preparing To Ascend Into
The Mighty Cloud Which Singly Hung From This Poor
Heaven*

so when she lay beside me
sleep's town went round her
and wondering children pressed against the high
    windows
of the room where we had been

so when she lay beside me
a voice, reminded of an old fashion :
    ' What are they saying ?
    of the planets and the turtles ?
    of the woodsman and the bee ? '
but we were too proud to answer, too tired to care
    about designs
    ' of tents and books and swords and birds '

thus does the circle pull upon itself
and all the gadding angels draw us in
until I can join her in that soft town where the bells
split apples on their tongues
and bring sleep down like a fish's shadow.

'O SHE IS AS LOVELY OFTEN'

O she is as lovely often as every day; the day following the day . . . the day of our lives, the brief day.

Within this moving room, this shadowy oftenness of days where the little hurry of our lives is said . . . O as lovely-often as the moving wing of a bird.

But ah, alas, sooner or later each of us must stand before that grim Roman Court, and be judged free of even such lies as I have told about the imperishable beauty of her hair. But that time is not now, and even such lies as I told about the enduring wonder of her grace, are lies that contain within them the only truth by which a man may live in this world.

O she is as lovely-often as every day; the day following the day . . . the day of our lives, ah, alas, the brief day.

'WHILE THE SUN STILL SPENDS HIS FABULOUS MONEY'

While the sun still spends his fabulous money
For the kingdoms in the eye of a fool,
Let us continue to waste our lives
Declaring beauty to the world

And let us continue to praise truth and justice
Though the eyes of the stars turn black
And the smoking juice of the universe,
Like the ruptured brain of God,
Pours down upon us in a final consecration

' O MY LOVE THE PRETTY TOWNS '

O my love
The pretty towns
All the blue tents of our nights together
And the lilies and the birds glad in our joy
The road through the forest
Where the surly wolf lived
And the snow at the top of the mountain
And the little rain
Falling on the roofs of the village
O my love my dearest
There is only room for our wonder
And the light leaning winds of heaven
Are not more sweet or pure
Than your fingers on my cheek
O my love my dearest
There are larks in our morning
And the lovely grace of your voice
And the flowers on the banks of the river
And the butterflies
And the whirling-mad
Butterflies!

'FROM MY HIGH LOVE I LOOK AT THAT POOR WORLD THERE'

From my high love I look at that poor world there;
I know that murder is the first prince in that tribe.

The towering sucking terror . . .
Schoolboys over whom the retching crows sing.
No, there is no lack of hell in that mad nest.
Gray horns hoot dismally in skeleton paws . . .

There is a little inn in the valley.
I wet my finger and put it to the wind;
Death whistles at his pitiless fun.

On the innwall I tack our two hearts;
Let not the bullets go through one before the other.

' O WHEN I TAKE MY LOVE OUT WALKING '

O when I take my love out walking
In the soft frosted stillness of this summer moon

Then are the mysteries all around us
O what can I say !
    the ever-known, the ever-new
    like her they seem
O lully, lullay
    only this little moment is real
Here at the edge of the world
    and the throne. The rest's a lie
    which shadows scheme.

Now gentle flowers are awash on the sleeping hill
And as I bend to kiss her opened lips
O then do the wonders and the sparklings seem
A shabby tinsel show for my dear queen.

CREATION

Wherever the dead are, there they are and
Nothing more. But you and I can expect
To see angels in the meadowgrass that look
Like cows —
And wherever we are is paradise
   in furnished room without bath and
   six flights up
Is all God ! We read
To one another, loving the sound of the s's
Slipping up on the t's and much is good
Enough to raise the hair on our heads, like
   Rilke and Wilfred Owen.

Any person who loves another person,
Wherever in the world, is with us in this room —
Even though there are battlefields.

'O NOW THE DRENCHED LAND WAKES'

O now the drenched land wakes;
Birds from their sleep call
Fitfully, and are still.
Clouds like milky wounds
Float across the moon.

O love, none may
Turn away long
From this white grove
Where all nouns grieve.

RELIGION IS THAT I LOVE YOU

As time will turn our bodies straight
In single sleep, the hunger fed, heart broken
Like a bottle used by thieves

Beloved, as so late our mouths meet, leaning
Our faces close, eyes closed —
Out there . . .

    Outside this window where branches toss
In soft wind, where birds move sudden wings . . .
Within that lamed air, love, we are dying

Let us watch that sleep come, put our fingers
Through the breath falling from us

Living, we can love though dying comes near
It is its desperate singing that we must not hear

It is that we cling together, not dying near each
    other now

'WHEN ALL THAT CHANGES IS THE WORLD'

When all that changes is the world,
Growing further away from every grace and good,
How then this change we feel in one another?

When those we love find breath a wound,
And curse against the very sun for giving light,
How then this doubt we feel in one another?

O ours is the change which flowers discover at morning!
O ours the doubt of the waters at their priestly moving!

WONDERFULLY LIFE O WONDERFULLY LIVING HEART

The stars in their wanton liveries
Wobble at the marriage-board of God,
As I put my arms around her.

I mean to wake the bellman
Of her sweets O of her tumbling moist hair
And I'll have every bell in the world ringing !

The happy flocks of our shepherd whisper
A lullaby to the silvery companies of heaven,
As I place myself above her.

I move through the room of this wonder
Of this purity O of this garden-running dear grace
And every proud song in the world is singing !

'LITTLE BIRDS SIT ON YOUR SHOULDERS'

Little birds sit on your shoulders,
    All pure and white.
Little birds sit on your shoulders,
    All lovely bright.

Men and times of evil,
    Nothing more is right.
Little birds sit on your shoulders,
    And sing me through the night.

' WHERE MY STAG-ANTLERED
LOVE MOVES '

Where my stag-antlered love moves
Across your warmspringing hills
In lengthening music to enter your cave
Is my world

Where my wet coin bears the stamp
Of an architecture as incredible
As His in Whose image it is

TO SAY IF YOU LOVE SOMEONE

O pretty village . . . aye, mine own home . . .
Lamps as yellow as ancient birds . . . here my
Love is . . .
Her breasts grow roses under my hands . . .
Her shoulders have the mark of my teeth upon
    them . . .
God, jewel the wind to a softer key
That her sleep be ornamented round
As halls the angels splendor in . . .
For we are tired in the green tall play
Of our bodies . . .
And she lies so warm and sweet in my arms

O all the bright summer . . . chamber
Of our kingdom . . . here my maleness
Had its wild design . . . joyful in the land
Of that strangest farmer . . .
A savage wonder made our every climate sing . . .
O God, such is the hospitality of my love
That the husbands of the great mysteries
Built cities near our bed,
And their white chaste daughters spun cloth
That we might be seemly clothed
When we turn from our dazzling occupation.
For soon we are going to sleep

'O SLEEPING LAY THE MAIDEN SNOW'

O sleeping lay the maiden snow
Upon the branches of the city
And oh my love was warm beside me

O nearer came the rush of dark wings
Over the dreams of my people
And oh my heart was full of their pain

O sleeping lay the maiden snow
Upon the bitter roofs of the world
But ah ! my love was safe in my arms

IN JUDGMENT OF THE LEAF

And we were speaking easily and all the light
    stayed low
Within your eyes; I think no equal glass has since
    been ground:
My love was looking through the throng that gave
    you mind.

We were quiet as the stars began to ride the billows;
And watching them we took an only mortal stair.
We wandered up the stable rays, were startled, lost
In a child's land whose stars are glory of jangling
    buoys,
Gunned by the froth of eternity and space.

Something snapped a twig at a distance from us:
It seemed real: a bird called its little bonfire of
    sound:
Thickets flamed with the trial of a leaf in the night.

Gentle hands were warm, scared within my hands;
    the moment's
Church wavered through Time's dripping tapers . . .
    was torn away. Suddenly
We knew that we could not belong again to simple
    love.

I saw your opening eyes reject the trade of tiny things
And I reasoned that the whole world might lie naked
In the earth of your eyes, in easy wonder building a new
    god.

THE CHARACTER OF LOVE SEEN AS A SEARCH FOR THE LOST

You, the woman; I, the man; this, the world:
And each is the work of all.

There is the muffled step in the snow; the stranger;
The crippled wren; the nun; the dancer; the Jesus-wing
Over the walkers in the village; and there are
Many beautiful arms about us and the things we know.

See how those stars tramp over heaven on their sticks
Of ancient light: with what simplicity that blue
Takes eternity into the quiet cave of God, where Caesar
And Socrates, like primitive paintings on a wall,
Look, with idiot eyes, on the world where we two are.

You, the sought for; I, the seeker; this, the search:
And each is the mission of all.

For greatness is only the drayhorse that coaxes
The built cart out; and where we go is reason.
But genius is an enormous littleness, a trickling
Of heart that covers alike the hare and the hunter.

How smoothly, like the sleep of a flower, love,
The grassy wind moves over night's tense meadow:
See how the great wooden eyes of the forest
Stare upon the architecture of our innocence.

You, the village; I the stranger; this, the road :
And each is the work of all.

Then, not that man do more, or stop pity; but that he be
Wider in living; that all his cities fly a clean flag . . .
We have been alone too long, love; it is terribly late
For the pierced feet on the water and we must not die now.

Have you wondered why all the windows in heaven were
                broken ?
Have you seen the homeless in the open grave of God's
                hand ?
Do you want to acquaint the larks with the fatuous music
                of war ?
There is the muffled step in the snow; the stranger;
The crippled wren; the nun; the dancer; the Jesus-wing
Over the walkers in the village; and there are
Many desperate arms about us and the things we know.

'DO I NOT DEAL WITH ANGELS'

Do I not deal with angels
When her lips I touch

So gentle, *so warm and sweet* — falsity
Has no sight of her
O the world is a place of veils and roses
When she is there

I am come to her wonder
Like a boy finding a star in a haymow
And there is nothing cruel or mad or evil
Anywhere

'AS WE ARE SO WONDERFULLY DONE WITH EACH OTHER'

As we are so wonderfully done with each other
We can walk into our separate sleep
On floors of music where the milkwhite cloak of
    childhood lies

Oh my love, my golden lark, my soft long doll!
Your lips have splashed my dull house with print of
    flowers
My hands are crooked where they spilled over your
    dear curving

It is good to be weary from that brilliant work
It is being God to feel your breathing under me

A waterglass on the bureau fills with morning . . .
Don't let anyone in to wake us

' THE SEA IS AWASH WITH ROSES '

The sea is awash with roses O they blow
Upon the land

The still hills fill with their scent
O the hills flow on their sweetness
As on God's hand

O love, it is so little we know of pleasure
Pleasure that lasts as the snow

But the sea is awash with roses O they blow
Upon the land

THE GREAT BIRDS

A gentle wind blows in from the water. Along the bank great birds are majestically striding. It is morning.

Far out there are boats. Far, far out on that crumbling blue shelf . . . toy swans slowly, slowly moving their honey-clotted wings. It is morning. Morning . . . and as every morning is, it is the first morning . . . *the first morning ever to come to this world.*

Morning . . . the land and sea and heavens! O everything hushed and cleaned by the wonder of it! As slowly, slowly the great birds wheel up . . . O everything still and waiting . . . until at last they are above the village . . . Above the soft golden blur of houses and bridges, O our two hearts turning slowly, slowly about up there!

And the boats . . . they are coming nearer! Now we can see the tumbling soft glitter of fish on their decks. And now, one of the fishermen, seeing us, waves, calls a greeting. And the birds, the great birds! ah now they are wheeling and diving close in over the water . . .

A strand of your hair brushes across my cheek.

How much better for the world had nothing else ever happened in it.

THERE ARE NOT MANY KINGDOMS LEFT

I write the lips of the moon upon her shoulders. In a temple of silvery farawayness I guard her to rest.

For her bed I write a stillness over all the swans of the world. With the morning breath of the snow leopard I cover her against any hurt.

Using the pen of rivers and mountaintops I store her pillow with singing.

Upon her hair I write the looking of the heavens at early morning.

— Away from this kingdom, from this last undefiled place, I would keep our governments, our civilization, and all other spirit-forsaken and corrupt institutions.

O cold beautiful blossoms of the moon moving upon her shoulders . . . the lips of the moon moving there . . . where the touch of any other lips would be a profanation.